Bavaria and Beer

by

Paul Riedel

Bavaria and Beer

History and Taste

by

Paul Riedel

Paul Riedel

Being an artist is not only a profession, but also a constant struggle against the currents of society. I experienced this in my early career years.

In my political views, protesting against the oppression of homosexuals was my constant companion. Equally important were animal rights and environmental protection. The more you learn from history, the more you want to correct in the one short lifetime you have. The path to fulfilling my goals led me to an awakened sense of enjoyment and a wish to liberate society from the negative marketing and overreach of the monopolists of the beer world. As a beer sommelier, I ask myself [the question], to what extent may I consume alcohol and offer it to third parties with a clear conscience? Alcoholism is a clearly defined disease according to the ICD-10, but how does one deal with social drinking?

Questions like these preoccupied me as I shaped my path of enjoyment. In my city tours, I see it as my mission to convey this to my guests.

I completed training as a sommelier to ensure a professional background on this issue. The training was more extensive than I expected and reinforced my views. I developed my concept in Brussels in 2006, recognising the bad reputation that accompanied beer. Beer drinkers were socially [seen as] of lesser standing than wine or even Scotch drinkers. Women who drink beer suffer even more than men from malicious gossip.

Beer contains less alcohol, less sugar and even has vitamins and other beneficial properties, compared to wine and Scotch. But nobody cares.

In the course of my investigation of the product I realised that beer has a long history that bears telling. In this way was born my quest, my enthusiasm for this beverage and I discovered the healthy pleasure of drinking beer.

It was not uncommon for me to have guests turn up for my city tours who were already drunk or boasting that they still had a hangover from the day before. It is precisely such people who struggle to appreciate the value of my tours. What was lacking all the more was a concept for beer presentation, which should also motivate a beer drinker to a new perspective of the experience.

However, a professional sommelier does not drink during working hours; he only tastes in small sips.

My goal is to help everyone to be in the instant, to gain the most enjoyment, to experience unforgettable moments.

In my presentation I address all your senses, because if you are satisfied with the day, you will not forget it so quickly, will you?

Give my method a go and add more pleasure to your life.

It all started with a little goat

Mythology has always fascinated me. Even as a child, my companions were the many heroes and gods from mythology, such as Thor, whose main pastime was boozing and guzzling. In my generation, you were only considered a man if you behaved the same way. Here I held bad cards because I did not conform to the ideal.

According to the story, the god Thor had a nanny-goat named Heidrun. An infinite supply of beer and mead could be suckled from her teats. Other sources record that she also brought mead for fallen heroes, but either way, she provided fun and enjoyment.

Thor's chariot was pulled by two goats, and dear Heidrun was always with them. She ate from the Larad tree, a relative of Yggdrasil, and from it she produced her beer and mead.

I chose Heidrun as my companion in this book because animals have something that is missing in our society: moderation. This is not a luxury, especially when it comes to beer, but something worth striving for.

Whether in eating, drinking, our obsession with obtaining the very latest in mobile telephone technology or exploiting the planet, we have lost all moderation and are struggling with the consequences.

Heidrun ensured unrestricted access to mead and beer. The two male goats were eaten by the thunder Gott for dinner every night, and then the bones were covered with their skins, and the goats were resurrected. This magical regeneration theme is repeated in many fairy tales and legends, such as the Greek legend of Jason and the Golden Fleece, the land of milk and honey or the story of the "The Self-Replenishing Food Table" that would deck itself with food on command.

In ancient times, eating and drinking well was the prerogative of the gods. They recognised their special position. Modern man wants to feel like a god, but we see from the problems of our time that over-indulgence only makes us sick. We are not gods, and our food and drink are not regenerated by miraculous pets.

You see, Heidrun fits perfectly here as my companion. She gives special hints, comments, and recipes. Therefore, my request to you, dear Reader be moderate and respect all living beings, even humans.

Preface

On my way to Canada, I stopped off in Munich for a job. Intrigued by the local history and tradition, I remained here and devoted myself to the precious Bavarian culture.

So, it was a coincidence that I came to Bavaria in 1984, but good fortune that I found my second home here.

At that time, I was dreaming of a future in Toronto and beer was far from my thoughts.

In the eighties, whisky was in vogue, and in discos it was important to have gaudy cocktails in your hand. I'll get to those drinks with umbrellas and fuss later. At the beginning of the eighties, we were cool. It's hard to imagine why, but that's also why I'm writing this book, isn't it?

In our current world of electronic media, social media, and superficial contact exchanges, people look firstly at a profile picture. They swipe quickly left or right and look for the next profile, mostly oblivious that they have swept to one side the best partner candidates in the process. Our court jester Prangl (Am Karlstor), as a love messenger, would have become horribly sad in the process.

Back then, we certainly didn't have a profile picture. With our hairstyles and weird gear, we would have been more likely to get a spot in a freak show from our photos than an invitation on a date. But with our hairspray, we were responsible for some of the hole in the ozone layer. Scientists will calculate this for us one of these days.

We revealed ourselves through our drinks. Expensive drinks signalled, "I'm too fine and too expensive a date for you." Colourfully decorated drinks in huge glasses belonged to wallflowers; they demonstrated either "I'm funny and nobody knows it" or "Help, I'm on my own again". I usually gave such fellows a wide berth. Gä,[1] they weren't my thing.

The really cool guys drank Johnnie Walker Black Label. And the best thing about it was that we couldn't get drunk on it, because it was so expensive that at the beginning of our careers, we could afford at most one drink a night. With that in hand, we would strut around for a long time and the dating worked great.

I don't want to be a telltale, but some of my acquaintances would pick up a glass left by a stranger and try to give suspicious waiters the slip all evening.

I don't want to just talk about the old times. But it illustrates why I came to love this special part of Germany and its cuisine so much. I give here a collection of my language skills, local superstitions, organisation of beer parties and how to understand and love Bavaria with any cultural background, be it for private or business purposes.

---

[1] In the Bavarian dialect this means nothing but reinforces the statement.

Bavaria

Reichsdeputationshauptschluss is the name of the biggest change on the European map, which was carried out by the Corsican Napoleon Bonaparte.

In August 1802, a commission convened to bring about the Peace of Lunéville.

Long negotiations followed, and, as always in history, after the numerous wars, men sat together to count the money. Forty-seven imperial cities were united in an instant to form Bavaria, Baden, and Württemberg.

Like the Borgs (in Star Trek), the commission assimilated them all. Languages and cultures were ignored, and so the colourful mixture of today's Bavaria was created.

On top of that, Napoleon Bonaparte stepped on the toes of the church. With secularisation, he incorporated the high monasteries ruled by bishops. Here, cities like Regensburg and Salzburg became part of Bavaria. Later, Salzburg was given back to Austria, but that's another chapter. Napoleon formed a confederation with the three new lands against the Habsburg family.

Emperor Franz II of Habsburg then laid down his crown in 1806; that was the end of almost nine centuries of the Holy Roman Empire of German Nations. Thus began the Bavarian Kingdom under Maximilian I.

We advertise diversity, because everywhere in Bavaria people speak differently and maintain their own folk costumes and traditions. Until 1806, Bavaria itself was far from finding a common identity, and now they are losing it yet again.

When Bavaria was proclaimed a kingdom in 1806, many of its inhabitants raised their eyebrows and harboured doubts about the nobility that wanted to consolidate itself. Certainly, the Wittelsbach family had been here for more than seven hundred years, but the status of the family had many ups and downs. It was shortly before a popular resistance to French interference when Maximilian realised that he had to act. He used the wedding of his son, Louis I, for identity building in the country. Traditional costumes from the baroque era, which had just been abandoned, came from everywhere (more or less as Sunday dress) and were paraded in front of the newly married couple, Ludwig I from Zweibrücken and Therese of Saxony.

Those who come to Munich are surprised at my enthusiasm for the "wonderful architecture". Yes, the years of war are hard to miss. The architecture that emerged after the destruction is worthy of discussion. This one does not show much of the royal heritage and the so-fabulous past. Everywhere you can see how diligently work has been done to restore the special atmosphere and rebuild local hospitality.

First impressions

Customs in Bavaria have great importance, and this is what is presented to the world in advertising brochures showing traditionally incorrect busty young women in dirndls serving overflowing tankards of beer. It really has *fei²* nothing to do with traditional costumes.

---

² "Fei", means nothing. This is just our dialect in Bavaria, and when we speak English, we use it anyway. Disregarding, that nobody understands.

Men in lederhosen tap their feet with curious elegance. That is *fei* not a Schuhplattler (flat shoes dancers) dance either.

And in the distant mountains, only men blow the alphorn. As if women had no lungs, bah!

Yes, these instruments are popular in Bavaria, but nowhere else in Germany.[3]

When people from other countries look through such brochures and relate with tears in their eyes how Grandma or Grandpa emigrated from Germany, we must correct a lot of false information.

Within the country, there are huge differences in traditional dress and customs.

Especially obvious in Bavaria are the hats. The hats of the women have floral decoration, while hunting trophies adorn the men's headgear. Today they are still to be seen being sported at the *Kocherlball* or Cooks' Ball.

The tuft of chamois hair ornamenting the men's hats, is striking. Many spend vast sums on it, not knowing that chamois hair is shorter, and buy expensive horse mane. Which is longer, but not rare.

Men of the country are world-famous for their leather breeches. According to some historians, lederhosen have existed in Europe since the 15th century. I have to correct my colleagues slightly on this point: even 5,000 years ago, Ötzi was already wearing leather breeches. Since one never washes these garments, I hope that the scientists put this

---

[3] Bavaria is part of Germany first since 1871

on the credit balance for us to offset our aerosol damage of the eighties.

Leather production requires a lot of water, so Spain and France, because of their proximity to the coast, were eminently suitable to produce the noble material.

Sans-culotte[4] was the name of the French clothing, which were workers' ankle-length pantaloons, and which have also been adopted in the current leather breeches fashion. They have no decorations or ornate embellishments, as some know-it-alls wear in beer tents nowadays. The breeches were cut roomily because they should stay with their owner for his whole life. You need room to grow, especially if you like beer, around the tum. The ornaments were instead reserved for the nobility, who did not wear goatskin or pigskin. They dressed in the skins of the animals they hunted, like the stag or chamois. Whether nobility or the rank and file, no one wears underpants with them.

Anyone buying leather breeches for the Oktoberfest is very much mistaken because real Munich people prefer jeans. We all know that even with expert waiters, it happens that beer is spilled on the fine loden or leather, and it is difficult to clean.

The new generation after COVID is a bit freer with their money. They pretend to be very traditional in their too-tight leather pants. Later, they auction off the greasy costume on the internet.

---

[4] Aristocrats called that way the working class who did not wear *culottes*.

There is also a shorter version of the leather breeches, which the Alpine area has made popular. This includes the *Wadelwärmer*, or calf warmers, if you want to wear the outfit correctly. In the Alps, clothes must be tough and for that this garment is perfectly suited. You will notice that the dirndl has an apron. This, as well as the blouse, changed several times, but not the dress. Underwear came much later.

One dresses here from head to toe according to local traditions, and so there is a matching shoe for this. It is called *Haferlschuh*: (like a half-shoe) but depending on the region also called *Bundschuh* or *Schützenschuh*. With the shoelaces fastening at the side, it is the most popular. There are variants with upper closure, but these are not in keeping with the local custom.

The Bavarian *Haferlschuh* was designed in 1803 and since then it has lost none of its popularity. They are also worn by the famous *Schuhplattler* (performers of a traditional Bavarian dance. The word *Schuhplattler* has its origins in the fact that the dancer strikes the soles of his shoes (*'Schuhe'*) with his hands held flat (*'platt'*), and *Schäfler* (barrel makers).

Women's shoes are hardly described in our traditions, because our ladies always come up with something and follow fashion trends. Even the famous dirndl is barely over a hundred years old and our king, Ludwig II, never saw it. It became popular at the end of the 19th century in urban areas, and then its popularity grew.

We drape our bandanas or tie them around our necks. I have been wearing this for many years and think it is very elegant.

We should also mention the charivari, a silver necklace with medallions and charms from different regions.

A nice tradition here; you can find the charivari in almost all trendy stores. Not only men wear it, but also women. If you really want to belong, you should also decorate your charivari with the medallions of the places you have visited.

Our favourite king, Ludwig I.

At the beginning of the 19th century, when Ludwig I (also known as Louis I) went from being a prince to a king, leather trousers were also extremely common in France.

Clothes make the man: our King Ludwig I already knew that. Many Bavarians like to suppress the fact that our favourite king came from France or, to be more precise, from Strasbourg. But that's because we like to have him just for ourselves. But don't worry, we love our "French neighbours" with all our hearts.

If you visit the Residenz in Munich or the Nymphenburg Palace, you will come across the most beautiful portraits of the king. His facial features reveal that he was an extremely charming man. Women would be overcome with adoration as he walked down the street, and his charm was his fortune as well as his undoing. Because of his many love affairs, including with the infamous Lola Montez, and his administrative problems, he was forced to abdicate in 1848. Lola was exiled to New York. A real "devil woman", she interfered in politics and particularly aroused the ire of society by consuming tobacco products in public or even carrying a riding whip. Her portrait can be seen at Nymphenburg Palace in the Gallery of the Beautiful.

An economic debacle resulted from the Beer Revolution in 1844, when Ludwig had to give in to popular protests and reduce the price of beer by ten percent. But this was not the only beer revolution in the country. Another followed in 1888 and even, more recently, on 12 May 1995, when it became known as the Bavarian Beer Garden Revolution. When the price isn't right, the people speak up.

Through King Ludwig I was born the first train line in Bavaria (and Germany), the wonderful classicist architecture of nineteenth-century Munich and some Bavarian traditions, such as, for example, the Oktoberfest. Its main architects were Klenze and Seidel. Busts of both gentlemen, who were buried in the South Cemetery, can be seen at Gärtnerplatz.

The first Oktoberfest took place on 17 October 1810, with a horse race. Ludwig I passed on the values he learned from his father, Max Joseph, to his son Maximilian II, who would go on to become the first Bavarian king to wear a traditional costume with Bavarian pride. In the Oktoberfest Museum the events can be followed in the various presentation rooms. Our Oktoberfest Queen Therese from Saxony contributes to the history with a special detail, because the first beer in the country came from Saxony.

Since the time of Maximilian II, Bavarians have been strolling around in their finely decorated lederhosen, although many nowadays no longer know why, except for some traditional costume clubs, which have this knowledge of our historical background.

The traditional costume boom

The *Trachtenboom* began with Maximilian II in the middle of the 19th century and continues until today.

Trachtenvereine (traditional costume clubs) and shooting clubs take as their mission the preservation of customs. As early as the Middle Ages, the Bavarians organised a front against foreigners moving in. It was not about hatred of foreigners, as one sometimes reads in the press, but about customs and common values. Some have certainly turned that into xenophobia after all, but there are always some who fail to grasp the principle and "mouth off".

The first shooting clubs had been gathering citizens and peasants into a military team already since around the 16th century, even before the Thirty Years' War. Actually, *Trachtenvereine* are successors of *Schützenvereine*, which came into being in the 20th century. When looking at the names, it is noticeable that there is no longer an exact distinction between the two variants.

The *Gebirgsschützen* (mountain riflemen) also have an important position in Bavarian society. Many members of such clubs, even if they have scarcely started shaving yet, know how the *Gebirgsschützen* used to build up a defence line along the Rivers Loisach and Isar.

My first impression of the Bavarians was not their appearance alone, but their talkativeness. They dress finely and like to talk, regardless of whether you understand them.

You can find similar cultural associations all over Europe, and they do a lot to maintain local traditions. But still, we try to resist homogeneity, as is the case in Scotland (like many other British regions) and the Spanish Catalonia.

Christian Religions in Bavaria are inevitable, and consequently, the *cult* of St Mary is popular everywhere.

She is revered, especially in Bavaria, and almost every pious household will display a painting or a statue of the saint. This can be found throughout Bavaria, not just in Munich.

I learned about this root of the Land in 1986, when I was lucky enough to have met a friend who knew a lot about local history.

In the process, I visited various traditional costume associations, and once I even greeted the head of the Miesbach Traditional Costume Association on my show on Radio LORA in 2016. At the end of my own research, I discovered that lederhosen are not Bavarian any more than I am. (I am originally from Brazil.)

This cultural movement was rather directed against the Prussians. Many of the supposed defenders of culture don't know that because Maximilian II's wife was from Prussia. This also confuses things a bit.

Maria of Prussia was a resolute lady, and the alleged affair with Tambosi (according to popular myth, possibly the father of Ludwig II) showed that she was somewhat different from women's concept in Catholic Bavaria. Of course, the leadership of the government also wanted to show the foreign lady that we are equal and have traditions and also distinguish ourselves externally – by the costume.

The beginning

Europe is always changing and what many like to forget is that Bavaria is far older than Germany. One speaks of Bavaria as a state in the federation, but the beginnings before the Carolingian period are documented even as far back as the 5th century.

The land was always rather poor and grew through good relations rather than warlike conquests. But before we get to the Wittelsbachs, there were a lot of Frankish rulers around here.

The Bavarian Empire grew on a lineage from the tribe of Pipinid and Carolingian houses. Clearly, references to Charlemagne (king in the 8th century), who was elected emperor, can be found in the capital several times. Many confuse him with Charles V the Great, who was actually King of Spain. The latter is from the House of Habsburg, and he can also be found in the Alte Pinakothek in Munich in a painting by Titian from the 16th century.

The lack of imagination (and strange traditions) of families in the Christian era in giving names to children contributed to the fact that we always find a lot of Charles, Otto, and Louis (or Paul). Even the numbers (like Otto 1st, 2nd, 3rd) and bynames (like the handsome, the saviour or the brave) don't help much because they are repetitive. That's why I always put the century before the names, so you know who's being talked about.

This is how the country looks currently.

Bavaria of today, after secularisation, has seven government districts, based on the original states of Napoleon's time. For each one, there is a lion on the coat of arms. To understand this, it is necessary to grasp our cultural diversity. The first lions came with Agnes of the Palatinate in the 13th century. Everywhere in Munich you can see lions, and they are even the main theme in the collection "Munich Lion Parade", which was designed by many artists.

Upper Bavaria is in the south, with Munich as its capital, which is easy to remember. Lower Bavaria is to the northeast of it, with the seat of government in Landshut. It's also worth a visit. Augsburg, which we touched on earlier and which has the famous Fuggerei, at 500 years old the world's oldest social housing complex, for indigent Catholics, is in Swabia. This is to the west of Upper Bavaria.

In the middle of Bavaria are two states: Upper Palatinate and Lower Bavaria. That's where you find Regensburg, where I sometimes take guests. The three states (Upper Bavaria, Lower Bavaria, and Upper Palatinate) comprise Old Bavaria. Bavarian (in German Bairisch) is spoken here. Bairisch has many subtypes, and each state has its own dialect. Their inhabitants can hardly communicate with each other. But let's not be completely petty.

West of the Upper Palatinate is Middle Franconia, with Ansbach as the seat of government. Although Bavaria is more associated with beer culture due to the massive marketing of Oktoberfest, the Palatinate and Franconia are among the top five wine-growing regions in Germany.

To the north is beautiful Franconia, divided into Lower Franconia, with Würzburg as its capital, and finally Upper Franconia, with the famous Wagner Theatre in the capital, Bayreuth.

Each place has its own dialects, costumes, and peculiarities, but we are united in one matter: everyone likes Bavarian beer.

That means "a piece of charcoal alone does not burn well." or, in other words, "One cannot get ahead on one's own". No matter where you travel in Bavaria, you can feel the friendliness and bond. Yes, there is sometime a cursing person, but that is also part of the local panorama.

Famous roads crisscross the state: the Salt Road between Salzburg and Freising, which even contributed to the creation of Munich. Or the post-war tourist attraction, the Romantic Road from Würzburg to Füssen, enjoys worldwide fame. It should also be stressed that in addition to the Porcelain Road, there is also a Beer Road. The Bavarian Beer Road is a modern concept with a promising future., The idea of building a tourism trail along the hop fields was born. Starting in Ingolstadt, the trail currently runs through Neuburg-Schrobenhausen, where the asparagus comes from, Pfaffenhofen an der Ilm and Kelheim. With the boom in microbreweries, it is to be expected that a great deal will happen here in the coming years. Therefore, bear this in mind and come back to Bavaria so as not to miss these beautiful areas and attractions.

The Beer Road connects numerous breweries and museums (including the Ettal Monastery Brewery Museum) and demonstrates production techniques.

The beer garden culture

The bottom-fermented beer, Pils or Helles, with its amber tone and malty background is light and, as they say here, quaffable. Since this requires a low temperature to develop, it was not authorised to be brewed in the summer. It must not ferment above 15°C; otherwise, it is all ruined. Here again, the church has set two saints as markers. It was allowed to be brewed only between St Michael's Day, on 29 September and St George's Day, on 23 April.

In order that everything could be stored in a cool place, the brewers-built cellars that reached a depth of twelve metres.

These were filled with ice from the surrounding waters, and this had to last until September. Most of the cellars in Munich still exist. On top of the cellar, a shelter from the sun still had to be organised. Here the chestnut trees were pressed into service. They have a low root and a wide crown. Since later in summer the fruits may fall down in our beer cups, we carry our wooden coasters in our pockets to protect the noble drink.

The bar in the immediate vicinity of the cellar was easy to handle. Also, the after-supply was guaranteed. Some of these cellars still exist today, even if only as local names, such as Augustiner Keller, Hofbräuhaus Keller or the Paulaner Keller.

Everywhere our chestnuts blossom in pink and white in spring, and in autumn our horses and deer enjoy the fruits of the chestnut trees.

Shade for the beer and food for the hardworking animals. The brewers' steeds make quite an impression at the traditional Oktoberfest procession.

This brewing regulation had been in effect since the Thirty Years' War, well before the establishment of Napoleon Bonaparte's new Bavaria.

Maximilian I introduced a liberal trade for the breweries, and this then led to an escalation with the local innkeepers.

Greed is the mother of all scuffles, and so there was a spat when meals were served in the beer garden in 1811. The patrons were enjoying the cool under the trees, the pubs were empty, and landlords were going hungry. Immediately, our Maxl was approached by the restaurant owners. He finally issued the beer garden ordinance on 4 January 1812.

So, it is to be seen until today that our pretzels are always praised by nice waiters, be it at the Wiesn, in the Hofbräuhaus or in other beer gardens.

Sociable was the word for our first king. He was seen more often in the Markets than in the barracks. Bavaria was mostly a peaceful state. We had fewer troops, and in war we were rarely there.

You could buy your food from the innkeeper, or simply prepare it at home.

Some nice radishes, gherkins, sausage salad and Obatzda Bavarian cheese are the basic elements that the local people expect. Sure, we are cosmopolitan, and even with humus or shashlik it is okay. The main thing is that we buy the beer in the beer garden. Sharing with guests at the table is most welcome: with friendly chat about the world and if one asks if there is still a place free at the table, you willingly move up closer together.

The beer created in March will be ready for St George's Day, and then there is a break with all the brewing. Whether that's why the beer is called Märzen, I'm not quite sure yet.

The former Märzen is brewed less at present. The demands of society have changed. Our environment and food demand different stimuli.

Dark is drunk less than light, hoppy and tart instead of malty and sweet.

Clearly, the marketing of breweries is aimed too much at abnormal consumption, and here you have to think a bit about the extent to which you give in. The brewer wants to sell by the litre, but our stomachs hold only 1.5 litres.

According to sources, Märzenbier is usually only offered at the Oktoberfest.

Family breweries in Bavaria are very traditional, and that is why you can still find Märzen there.

The claim that lighter beers are currently in fashion, I think is very daring. Even most Americans can barely stand the Cool, Zero and Light. If you are looking for a milder option, in Bavaria you can find the alcohol free, and all beer gardens offer that.

An important branch of beer in the beer garden is Radler. Whether with lemonade, apple, or grapefruit spritzer, you can find this blend everywhere. Especially if you still have to drive or take care of children, you can join in the drinking with a clear conscience.

All kinds of cuisine to match the beer.

To enjoy beer with all your senses, you must not forget good food. A good mixture of herbs for salads is not difficult to make yourself. Although you can buy them ready-made in the supermarket, I recommend everyone discover their own taste.

I do buy supermarket herbs and mix them together, but in the process, I create my own composition: fewer nuts, more pepper, and be careful with salt.

Dried herbs in a sealed jar last six months without problems. Of course, you can store these herbs for years, but after a while they just taste like straw. Therefore, always document the shelf life on the bottom of the jar or on the lid. This is a good way to make your diet more balanced. If the herbs lie around untouched for too long, you know yourself that you should eat a little more salad.

Dried herbs are well known and often bought, but unfortunately rarely tasted. These contain essential oils, and with a few exceptions, you hardly smell anything. To bring this out, you would have to press them beforehand, mix them with salt, or dissolve them in oil (pickle). I prefer the salt mixture. Salt absorbs the oils well and has a longer shelf life.

I love to write down my recipes manually. In today's over-technological world, you tend to photograph and upload everything, save it, and then forget it.

The information overload is almost equal to our beer and food consumption. That's why I definitely recommend taking the time to relax and write down some of my tips for the kitchen, especially manually. Some people's handwriting was so unpractised that it resembled the dance of a spider who had fallen in ink and then drunkenly danced on paper.

Herbal blends are helpful for simple beer tasting, but it is important to note that salt should be enjoyed very moderately. Salt changes the flavour. Keep this in mind.

I use my various herb blends for salads and soups, but also to flavour cheeses and some appetisers. Herbs are more neutral than spices, like cardamom, nutmeg, or cloves. These herbs can also have a very exotic flavour for food pairing or beer tasting. I especially like to use them for my Christmas tastings. My recommendation is always to boldly taste ahead. We will be amazed at the variety of good tastes we discover.

Professional friends have learned this from me, and here is my herb mix for salads.

Herbs have magical properties in addition to their medicinal effects. I'm pretty pragmatic, so my belief in magic is very limited. But I have found that some health properties, due to our limited knowledge of herbal effects, are more easily explained by magic. The lifespan of essential oils varies, and one should be familiar with them to be able to design a long-lasting blend.

This is likewise what happened to the mistress of herbalism, Hildegard of Bingen. Born in the late 11th century, she lived long – let us hope healthily – until the age of 81. She was the discoverer of hops. Without this woman, we would have only had sweet beer until today. But the church people were jealous of her (what exceptional behaviour, ha-ha). With the fear of a possible accusation of witchcraft due to her visions, she had to assert herself in the world of men. She was a contemporary of Friederich Barbarossa, who was indirectly the founder of Munich.

She discovered that the bitter substance of hops delayed the rotting of beer (and other processes). It's a preservative in that sense. I recommend that anyone interested in alternative methods for enjoying beer investigate herbalism a bit. I use rosemary, elderberry, lavender, and others in some of my blends, which I cover later in the book.

In addition to their floral aromas and invigorating or calming properties, these and other herbs also provide a pleasant balance to alcohol and sugar.

Enjoying intelligently increases life expectancy!

But salt was the beginning.

With or without traditional costumes, Bavaria is sunny and beautiful. We enjoy our beer garden with friends and strangers. I speak deliberately of "ours" because after forty years I have found Bavaria to be my second home. It has not been an easy path, but with a rewarding destination.

Salt brought a lot of attention to Bavaria. The Salzburg Salt Road to Freising (Munich in the north) was so famous that the administrator of the Luneburg Salt Road, Frederick Barbarossa, sent his cousin as duke to the place, as yet unnamed, which became Munich. Through Henry the Lion, the cosmopolitan city with a heart, Munich, came into being. Henry the Lion can still be seen immortalised in the Old Town Hall as a bronze statue.

Emperor Frederick I was also called Barbarossa. He took part in the second and third crusades and is particularly important in Bavaria's history. He brought to us the Wittelsbach family. It is still a mystery to me how he administered Bavaria from Luneburg. The distances were not only very long, but also dangerous. He even interfered in the art of brewing here in the region, repriming brewers from Augsburg. In 1156, he instructed the bailiff of the then bishopric of Augsburg to impose a five-guilder fine if bad beer was served.

Many do not think of such details, but Augsburg has belonged to Bavaria only since the secularisation, as well as Salzburg. Before that, Augsburg belonged to the bishopric of Mainz.

The tradition of dukes, kings and emperors has been written down since 556 A.D. We know that Garibaldi I was the oldest documented king of Bavaria. But the empire, from Verona as far as Croatia, was called the Land of the Bavarians until Napoleon Bonaparte came.

Enough wandering into history—let's get back to salt.

You can do a lot with salt. Combined with meat, plus imagination, spices and herbs, the many Bavarian sausage variations are created. Everything that you do not want or should not see is crushed beyond recognition and mixed with salt and turned into sausages. There was no refrigeration and to preserve the fruits and harvest there was only salt, vinegar or drying out, smoking or sunning.

It may be that many claim to like meat, but except for steaks, what ends up on the plate doesn't even remotely look like meat.

The taste of meat is packed under so many spices that even vegetarian versions are hard to distinguish.

As a vegetarian by nature, it was difficult for me at first in Bavaria. Everyone around me said that you can't have a Bavarian snack without brawn and black pudding. So, I bought some and reluctantly chewed on the stuff and swallowed it. Today I know that that was a load of rubbish. You can live excellently here even as a vegetarian.

Vegetarian used to be a dirty word, but fortunately things have changed.

Back in the eighties, I was also persuaded to try meatloaf. Admittedly, I found it not uninteresting, but my nose said no. So, I bought it for my friends and packed radish and turnip for myself.

If we look very objectively at our kitchen, the most popular products are those that are rotting. Cheese is made from on-the-turn milk, beer, with the fermentation of grain and wine, with fermenting fruits and the best breads are baked with sourdough.

Those who knew my three grannies know that everything that is not consumed is pickled, packaged, or made into soup.

Fruits are pickled, in a Rum Topf (fruits preserved in run and sugar), liquor or simply processed as compote or jam. Although my grandmothers come from completely different corners of the world, housewives or househusbands are similar everywhere in the household. Brazil, Angola, or Germany, everywhere according to the motto: Nothing is thrown away but saved as a precaution for a rainy day.

But until I get to my Bavarian plate, we have to have bread, and the good househusband knows how to bake his own bread.

All our food that you do not prepare yourself, that comes from the supermarket or ordered in, contains far too much salt. This is to improve the shelf life. That's why I recommend hiring a chef for your own tasting or getting into the kitchen yourself and making sure "no one is salting your soup". Besides the need for preservation, it is also tradition that always motivates us to salt. Steaks, grilled foods, chips - everything gets over-salted. I would love to lecture all my guests on the downside of consuming salt, but who wants to be the killjoy. A very useful remark here is, that we don't use as much sea salt as we used before. Sea salt has a lot of nutritional advantages.

Good mixed herbs replace the saltiness, and they don't interfere with the flavours of the beers.

Bread and Pretzels

Beer and bread superficially have the same basic ingredients, namely grain, leavening agent, and water.

Both are healthy and very original, and bread as a staple food contributes to a complete diet. The DGA (Deutsche Gesellschaft für Ernährung e. V., German Nutrition Society) recommends consuming at least 30 grams of fibre daily from whole grains, vegetables, legumes, and fruit.

This is present in dark bread, but there is not very much at all in white bread. The diversity of bread varieties in Bavaria is unique in the world, with more than 300 types. Black, wholemeal, multigrain, and mixed rye breads are among the typical regional bread varieties and are at the top of the popularity scale in the state.

On average, each man eats 158 g and each woman 111 g of bread a day. Perhaps the belief that bread makes you fat comes from its high carbohydrate content. Also, the new celiac disease (gluten intolerance), which has become known in society, somewhat confuses our approach to bread.

In history, we often suffer from naivety. Thus, when a finer and more elegant version of bread emerged in France, it was designated for the nobility. However, this sophisticated new creation had very little nutritional value and was even harmful to the intestines. White bread is basically poorer in vitamins and minerals than wholewheat bread.

Because it has more starch, it is unsuitable for diabetics and yes, it does encourage gaining weight. Industrially produced white bread often contains chemical additives such as bleaching agents or emulsifiers, which are put in to optimise colour, consistency, and shelf life.

These additives put a strain on the metabolism and can lead to long-term health problems.

Most sources I've used agree on this, and I adhere very closely to these guidelines, having been a diabetic myself for over twenty years.

The best guidance is found where you can find like-minded people. Therefore, vegetarians should seek recipes that cover the lack of protein.

Whether with sourdough, rye, wheat, or bread made from wheat and rye flour: the variety is great in Germany. However, the types of bread in Bavaria are something special.

After people discovered grain as food more than 10,000 years ago, they first prepared it as porridge or soup. Beer, in my opinion, would come later, but according to my assumption, bread came first.

Alcohol is far more complicated to produce than bread. We owe bread-making to the ancient peoples, whether Egyptians, Sumerians, or Mesopotamians. But mixing grains with water to make them softer is something most animals can do. Ravens, squirrels or even dogs do it. My garden raven, Olga, does it too.

Bread has been around in its present form for about 2,000 years. The ancient Romans invented the mill and the kneading machine, which increased the number of types of bread very rapidly. The basis for almost every loaf of bread is always the same. The different types of bread are created by an individual mixture of different flours, grains, and leavening agents, such as fat, sugar, fruits, or grains; there is hardly a limit to our creativity. Not to be ignored are the imaginative shapes, sizes, and decoration, especially in Bavaria, which gives us over three thousand types of bread. Almost 50 percent of Bavarian bread is open baked, and at the end of the production process, it has a characteristic round shape, called Leib. The manufacturing process clearly influences which type of bread comes out of the oven at the end.

Because of its importance for mankind, this baked good has not lost its appeal throughout history. At Easter, the Maundy Thursday bread with an Easter pancake drives away sinister spirits. The vernacular says, "You earn your bread or eat supper." (We didn't eat and work at the same time.) In Bavaria, instead of "snack," it is more meaningfully called "Brotzeit" the bread time. Every region also has its own flagship bread. The Bavarians are proud of their pretzels – "Brezn", which in the rest of Germany are called "Brezeln". Traditionally, they are eaten with either a veal sausage (Weiss Wurst) or Obatzda (cheese spread). For a Wiener (a frankfurter type sausage), the crusty brown bread is more appropriate.

Depending on whether you choose to visit a traditional bakery or venture into a modern one, Brezn (pretzels) must always be included in a beer tasting. Modern bakeries have their own charm, but they are certainly not my choice. In

Munich, some colleagues offer rolls for beer tasting. But I am not a fan of white bread. The white flour from the pretzel is enough for me.

At the Oktoberfest, we even have a giant version of the pretzel, the Wiesnbrezen (or Oktoberfest pretzel). But if you want to enjoy one in the meantime, get it at the bakery or in various restaurants. The pretzel available in Bavaria is salty; in neighbouring Salzburg, in various strange, sweet variants, which we look at askance, but we eat them anyway. Marzipan, sugar icing, Mozart kugel (a chocolate covered ball of pistachio marzipan and nougat), bacon or vanilla are some variants that we in Bavaria consider call into question the divinity of bread. I advise my guests to scrape off the coarse salt. Given the coronary stresses, and other side effects associated with salt, it's not a luxury.

The name of the pretzel comes from the Latin *brachium*, which translates to "arm" and is therefore a reference to the folded arms at prayer.

Our visitors stumble upon the term "Pfisterbrot". The bread comes from Ludwig Stocker's Munich Hofpfisterei, as the bakery chain is called; it was founded in 1331.

It supplies not only the capital and the surrounding area, but also many neighbouring towns in the region. By far the most popular among Bavarians are mixed rye breads. They are followed by mixed wheat breads and whole-grain breads in general. You'll look in vain for oat bread in the Free State of Bavaria, unless you have someone as familiar with the area as I am. For my beer tastings, I prefer the Bavarian platter.

Just pack the best of the house in a basket and serve it up in the beer garden or event space. Everything is certainly nicely decorated for events, but it's the same principle.

But in the beer garden we need more than just potato salad, for example, chicken or bratwurst from the grill. I usually bring my grilled vegetables, which makes some people smile.

I microwave the carrots for seven minutes and sprinkle them with some spices and my herb mix. They are always a hit.

Radi, turnips, horseradish, and pickled cucumbers, so you have something healthy, and then clearly you need to spice things up with Obatzda.

Everywhere in Bavaria, we like to ride our bikes, not just for the sake of the environment, but because we really enjoy nature. Try this. In this way the calories are reduced, and the beer tastes even better.

Original Obatzda to make yourself.

The ingredients in the recipe are calculated for four Bavarians or six inexperienced Obatzda eaters.

The Obatzda is quickly prepared in 15 minutes.

3 rlpe Camembert, 250 grams each.

½ Limburger (= 100 grams).

1 unsalted butter (= 250 grams)

1 dash of beer

Rose paprika powder

a pinch each of salt and black pepper

1 medium red onion finely diced.

Preparation

Remove the butter from the refrigerator at least half an hour before preparation.

Then mash the Camembert with a fork. Add butter and Limburger and continue to work into a paste. If the paste is too dry, add some beer.

And now get some pretzels and take a break.

Beer

If I were to list all kinds of beer here, there would be no end. Therefore, I concentrate on the Munich beers and some of my favourite homemade ones (known as craft beer).

My use of superlatives is very moderate, because mostly these are spread by the beer industry. I no longer speak of "the most popular", "the most typical" or "the beer everyone loves". In my experience, phrases with such predicates are just repeated parrot-fashion as a result of insidious persuasion from marketing campaigns of the large corporations.

In the face of the emerging movement of micro-producers, a certain distance from the monopolists is necessary.

I don't like serving half or whole litre beers, I prefer more moderate amounts. Such quantities are good for the producer sales because they reach more, but serving by the litre or half-litre means my guests have a reduced space in their stomach.

The determining factor for the type of beer is the original wort. This describes the proportion of dissolved ingredients originating from the malt. Malt sugar, minerals, vitamins, and wort are some of them.

Further classification of beer types includes the leavening agents used, as well as colour, flavour, and type of malt. Large-scale producers use top-fermenting and bottom-fermenting yeast in their brewing methods. Micro-producers use mixtures of these and other special varieties.

In Ancient Egypt beer brewing was a state monopoly. (Oops, yes, the Hofbräuhaus also belongs to the state of Bavaria, and so it is based on an ancient tradition.) Various clay tablets document the distribution of beer in society, from the pharaoh to the lowest construction worker. I deliberately do not use the word slave, firstly because there were none at that time, and secondly because the ancient Egyptians hardly knew Western Europe. Grave goods also prove the devotion and prestige of the product. Imagine waking up after millions of years and drinking your beer from the amphorae next to your own coffin ... Well ... there is something fresher here.

As you will have noticed, in Greece and Italy beer is less popular than in Germany and the Nordic countries.

This resulted from Roman propaganda. They considered beer to be a drink for barbarians. Unfortunately, it has remained that way and today hooligans and other people you would rather not invite to your home enjoy themselves as typical beer consumers.

Or does anyone know of a soccer match where they serve wine and champagne?

Beer and the land have been developing together since early antiquity. The ancient Babylonian King Hammurabi (1792–1750 BCE) established regulations to protect beer consumers. The innkeeper was paid in barley for serving beer; if it was so expensive that she took silver for it (too expensive beer), she was drowned. If a priestess visited or opened an inn, she would be burned at the stake, and beer adulterers would be drowned in their brew. If the king were ever to have visited our Oktoberfest, I would have loved to have been there. The brew was expensive, the priests ran most of the pubs, but you could hardly complain about the quality of the drink.

While searching for the origin of Bavarian beer, I came across some highly compelling material in Lower Saxony, in which lies the town of Einbeck. It's no secret that the Bavarians would have preferred beer to have been invented here in the countryside, but the Lord God wanted to give the out-of-towners a treat. Frederick Barbarossa, to whom we owe Munich, either founded Markt Einböck or was merely the first to mention it by name in a document. He did the same with our capital. In what is now called Einbeck, the brewing of beer was part of society, and there are even records that prove that beer was brewed there in the 14th century. According to the stories, in 1614, under Elector Maximilian I, the brewmaster Elias Pichler, from Einbeck, was hired to succeed Heimeran Pongratz at the Hofbräuhaus. Pichler successfully changed the beer, among other things, a remarkable achievement in the history of beer. Whether history really happened that way is doubted by some experts and confirmed by others. In any case, we know that Einbeck beer was too expensive to import. Therefore, it was a logical decision for one of the best dukes we have had to brew it here directly.

But I would like to mention something from our various ordinances for the distribution of beer and wine, because you can see that women were fundamentally disadvantaged. In 817 at the Council of Aachen, the rulers stated that, depending on the place, for monks decisively more beer-brewing was granted than for nuns. From the law one reads indirectly how much beer and wine was drunk in monasteries.

No wonder so many reports having encountered the Holy Spirit on several occasions. Admittedly, the beers of that time were far milder in alcohol content than those of today. For the more senior monks there were spicier brews, for novices was a beer named Conventus, a kind of milder beer.

When we talk about serving beer to minors in earlier generations, we should keep in mind that the beer of that time had only a few percent of alcohol and one measure was enough for the whole family. Our overconsumption of beer, touted by marketing agencies as masculine, cool, and normal, is, in my opinion, a crime against society. Diabetes, obesity, and gluttony are diseases created by strategies of producers and cloud the minds of consumers who, unfortunately, like sheep (or goats, sorry Heidrun) hardly notice how they are manipulated. In my work as a sommelier, I also have to keep a clear eye on whether a beer is served in the right measures. I would never offer a beer with a high alcohol percentage in large quantities. Enjoyment also has to be intelligent. Eating and drinking is fine, but what's too much is, after all, too much. Beer can be produced from almost all grains and herbs. In my selection for a Bavarian tasting, I have chosen the most locally popular, which can be found worldwide. But something still needs to be addressed, and that is our Reinheitsgebot.

Reinheitsgebot

"Wie das pier summer un winter auf dem Land sol geschenckt und prauen werden."

In order to understand the saying, I have to refer back to a chapter in beer history that is known to many, at least in Germany.

William IV of Bavaria and his brother Louis X ruled the country together at the beginning of the 16th century. At the Estates Day in Ingolstadt on 23 April 1516, the two noble men issued a decree on the purity of beer.

Oh, what? I don't want to spread rumours, but by chance, Munich came into money in the same year and was able to commission and pay for the dome of the Frauenkirche.

From then on, the brewed beverage was subject to a strict regulation, according to which it could then only be brewed from barley malt, water, and hops. Yeast came into play later. Definitions and superlatives in historical treatises always attract my attention. That is why I draw on various sources to understand why the decree was necessary. There have been more than enough misinterpretations in historical research.

Through the organised methods of the monasteries, they produced better beers than in private households and clearly, a larger quantity, through which they came into an additional income.

Political, religious, or personal interpretations always overshadow the truth, and, in my opinion, that is the case here as well.

Did the rulers care about the well-being of the people?

Even if I were to be accused of cynicism, I could scarcely believe that rulers ever cared about the nation. Then what was this really about?

A saying in folk history even became famous through poetry and song:

"Wheat for bread, barley for beer, oats for horses".

But wheat beer was especially important for Elector Maximilian I in the 17th century as a source of income. So, I deepened my research. The Wittelsbach protected the exclusive right to brew with wheat. As a result, the Wittelsbachers became monopolists of wheat beer. Shortly before the Thirty Years' War, Elector Maximilian I also acquired a brewer from Einbeck for the Hofbrau. This documents his business sense with beer in the best possible way.

Regents helped themselves to the beer penny in various chapters of history. This financial resource helped to build bridges, maintain armies, or fill the coffers after war. Control over the ingredients of beer appeared again and again in decrees and edicts.

Besides kings, emperors and other rulers, others queued up with their hats held out, waiting for the money. Among the most influential monopolists in the beer world, we count the church.

Most of the major beer producers find their roots in monasteries or brotherhoods. Of the current two out of six breweries at the Oktoberfest, Augustiner and Paulaner have just such an ecclesiastical background.

Assuming that brewing beer can be easily done at home and that this home brew would not be levied any tax, then here we have the first conflict of interest. Some of the sources in my research laid out a fascinating connection: the witch hunt and the beer monopoly.

It has been known that women, from ancient times, cared more about medical knowledge and religion than men. It is also documented from lore that they used various additional herbs in brewing beer. Wild rosemary and bog myrtle are just two of them. This background even led Hildegard of Bingen, in the 12th century to discover hops, which today are indispensable.

Representatives of the Purity Law persist with unnecessary fidelity to the mediaeval rulers, claiming that the Church had no influence on this decree. I am convinced that the Catholic upbringing of the two dukes and their worldview already had a hand in the decision.

Munich has actually had over seventy breweries in its history, compared to the paltry six we currently count here, a great loss for diversity and brewing culture. Of the remaining ones, three are already in the hands of international corporations, almost heralding the apocalypse of beer culture.

The industrialisation process has sacrificed the good quality content of beers to quantity. Vitamin B complex, microorganisms and ingredients of brewer's yeast are some of the positive elements that have been reduced or even completely filtered out to allow a uniform taste.

With the new craft beer movement, many young brewers are turning to old recipes or alternative ingredients. They are looking for perfection in the art of brewing rather than in the purity law, and they are bringing lost elements back into the product.

At the moment, such beers sometimes suffer from extreme hop aromas that drown out everything else. But this wave will soon subside, and other options will emerge.

Personally, I am against the purity law on principle. It limits creativity and offers no particular benefits to the product. Let's consider that if Hildegard von Bingen had not discovered hops as an additional ingredient, we would have to celebrate Oktoberfest with a rather tepid swill. As far as one sees as a rule the purity of the product, without chemicals, flavourings, preservatives, or flavour enhancers, I am all for it, but these precise agents were not the subject of the original regulation. We must also consider whether this regulation was not just a regulation against the women who brewed their beer outside the cities. It must not be forgotten that these women paid little or no tax and were not under the supervision of the churches and the state. They were therefore also an easy target for accusations of witchcraft.

Even when some historians confidently relay what they have learned, their point of view is not always logical. For logic requires free thinking, which does not always occur. They take the view that it was all about grain for bread.

Pilsner

Bavaria has excellent connections with Bohemia. We always see these on our lozenge flag. Indeed, the twenty-one diamonds, white and blue, originate from Bohemia. With the marriage between the Czech-Bohemian princess (daughter of Duke Frederick of Bohemia) and our Ludwig I of Bavaria in 1204, history connected both nations. For Ludmilla, it was her second marriage, and if the records are correct, her first husband was Count Adalbert III of Bogen. To avoid confusion, it should be considered that there was already another Ludmilla of Bohemia in the ninth century.

The lozenges on our coat of arms officially came to us as an inheritance with the death of Ludmilla's son (Albert IV of Bogen). Only then did the symbols pass to his half-brother Otto III of Bavaria, and thus to the Bavarian flag. Bohemia became part of the Austro-Hungarian Empire, and there the German language was also the official language for a long time.

Pilsen is located in Bohemia (Czech Republic) and Pilsner continues to be one of the most popular beers in Germany. The Pilsener, or Pilsner also has a different variety depending on the location. Four popular varieties are known: malty with a buttery note is the Bohemian, strong, hop aromatic is the Bavarian, the milder, hop aromatic and leaner variety is the North German and the strong hoppy is the American. This classification is not a valuation. After all, other local flavours exist. Good recipes always find improvements or modifications. In the middle of the 19th century in the city of Plzen (Pilsen) Joseph Groll, a Bavarian brewmaster in the newly built Czech brewery *Měšťanský pivovar Poličce* created the new type of beer. The brewery that commissioned him was struggling to gain a better reputation.

With yeast brought from Bavaria himself, the young brewmaster put his heart into it. The water from the area around Moravia (East Czech Republic), the local barley and the hops provided good conditions for the new brewed beverage. The new brewing technology from Bavaria led the brewmaster to produce the product at low temperatures. Stored in barrels in the cellar, the brew, lovingly composed, transformed. The result was golden blond, low in sulphur, slightly citrusy and mildly carbonated. These characteristics won over consumers in no time.

Its premiere was celebrated on St Martin's Day in 1842. The new beverage was christened Plzeňský Prazdroj, or Pilsener Urquell.

The Pilsner produces a lot of foam, which increases the finger sensitivity when tapping. Internationally recognised and often copied, it was decided in 2008 in the EU that Czech beer should be placed under the status of "protected designation of origin".

Pilsner must meet specified requirements, such as the exclusive use of selected Czech barley varieties.

Otherwise, the name must be changed.

Also, this is more or less another way of purity law, but I emphasise that I am not a proponent of it.

Helles

After the great success of Carl Linde's refrigerated machine in 1871, the way was paved for the production of bottom-fermented beers year-round.

In sommelier circles, the beverages resulting from bottom-fermenting yeast are generally classified as less aromatic than the top-fermenting varieties. Bottom-fermenting yeast unfolds at 4° to 9°C. In times without refrigeration, bottom-fermenting yeast could only be used during the cold season.

Until then, top-fermented beer was predominantly brewed. Top-fermented yeast unfolds at 12° to 19°C. The most common Munich full beer is filtered, golden, bottom-fermented, with dense foam, subtle malt, and a light citrus aroma. With an alcohol content of between 4.6 and 5.6 percent, it is light and, as they say in Bavaria, quaffable. Like all beers brewed according to the Reinheitsgebot, it is made from barley malt.

An almost young product. Brewed for the first time in 1894 by the Spaten brewery, this beer was initially accompanied by uncertainty. Thus, the drink was first sold to the neighbour to the north. Helles was finally tested in the first official bar in Hamburg. As is usual with good products, there are always disputes as to the originator, and this was also the case with Helles. According to another source, it was the brothers Ludwig and Eugen Thomass who released a Bohemian Pils original in 1895. The Bohemian Pils had been on the market in Bavaria since 1842 and was very popular. The Bohemian Pilsner is the root on which the Helle is based. In order to bring Helles to the market, it first had to be well tested. So that the name could be based on the biblical Thomas, the spelling of Thomas-Bräu with only one S was established.

It was then redirected in 1928 into a community of interest with Paulaner to form AG Paulaner Bräu, Salvator Brauerei and Thomas Bräu. It almost doesn't matter whether Thomas Bräu or Spaten is the originator, as both products were created almost in parallel. In any case, the Spaten-Helle was tested in Hamburg.

All Bavarian beers with an original wort content of 11 to below 16 percent belong to the genre of light full beers or lagers, Helles being one of them, clearly filtered in the barrel or matured in the bottle. Because of the filtering, sommeliers refer to them as Blanken beers (clear filtered), which I personally don't think is the best beer recommendation. They are certainly very drinkable and popular, but I prefer the cloudy versions because they are more satisfying.

Today's market presence of the pale is unmistakable. At the Oktoberfest, it's almost impossible to order anything else. Eyerolls and inventive insults greet an order of other types of beer, or even water. In Munich, Augustiner Edelstoff is considered the best of all pale beers, but that's only one of Munich's current seven regular breweries. Hofbrau is very popular and Löwenbräu with its beer gardens must also be mentioned. I like to be eclectic. Our youngest chick in the beer names from Munich is Giesinger-Bräu, which adds to the diversity.

Light beer harmonises perfectly with apple juice, natural lemonade, or pineapple juice. I usually mix in a ratio of one-third to two-thirds and served preferably no colder than 8°C in wide glasses to allow the drink to breathe well. As a very special treat, I boil lavender or rosemary. The result, which I mix with lemon juice and carbonated water and sweetened with a little honey, has been praised. It is important in such mixtures to avoid sugar.

Dark

Dark beer was considered the standard Bavarian brew until the end of the 19th century. To distinguish it from wheat beer (dark wheat beer), this was called red beer. It has an alcohol content of 4.5 to 6 percent, an original wort of 11 to 13 percent and is bottom-fermented. Brewing dark beer requires more sophisticated processing than most other varieties.

Roasted malt is responsible for the colour. As in all dark beers, roasting and blending of coloured malts is required. This produces a scratchy aftertaste. The brewers' challenge is to soften this taste so that the beer is more pleasant.

As a brewmaster's challenge, the head must be light despite the dark colour of the beer.

I avoid too much head in my beers. First, it's an impediment to the drink's ability to breathe, and whether it's as nice as advertised is open to long debate. Compared to pale beers, blends for dark beers are a bit more difficult because the beer has a stronger body. Blends can drown that out too much. Generally, I add as many additional fizzy drinks (sodas), teas or other non-alcoholic components to the beer until the alcohol content is below three percent. Even in the non-alcoholic version, beers are tasty but, quite honestly, far from as quaffable as the alcoholic versions. Darks should be tart and aromatic, but in the craft beer world, I've encountered many that almost overshoot the mark. Chocolate, caramel, and cherry are popular flavours that are interesting but also too seductive for alcohol consumption.

As a rule, a man should not consume more than 0.5 litres per week, and women, unfortunately, even less. This is what nutritionists and doctors recommend. Those who drink their half-litre every day should definitely have their liver checked.

In my tastings, I offer dark beer, usually with currant juice or spritzer. I avoid the ready-made spritzers because they usually contain too much white sugar and chemicals I don't like to have in my body. But a beer has as many calories as fizzy drinks, so a mix is just as harmful as a beer straight, just with less alcohol, which at least reduces that danger.

Other options for a healthy mix with dark beer, according to my research, are cherry spritzers, elderberry spritzers and black tea with honey. I realise that the average consumer, who has been conditioned for fifty years to drink beer straight, cringes at the idea of trying some blends, but I always say, "Who eats bread without toppings?" Beer is just liquid bread.

In terms of quantity, I recommend serving no more than 0.2 litres. Sure, some seniors will howl because they want to swill a whole litre, but a beer tasting should be aimed at enjoyment, not quantity.

At Christmas, I use some sweet and dark ingredients to make my warm beer recipe, which I highly recommend.

Wheat beer (Weissbier)

Wheat beer, also known as "white" beer, is one of the first types of beer that existed far in the past.

The name makes the interested connoisseur wonder why the colour of the beer is anything but white. This is purely due to pronunciation in dialects that couldn't distinguish between *Weiz* (wheat) and *Weiss* (white). This is easy to understand for anyone who has lived long enough and heard all the dialects. Bavaria and the wheat beer culture are inseparable. It is enjoyed in the rural beer gardens of the Alps, as well as in the lively brewhouses of Munich.

In the 16th century Duke Wilhelm IV granted the ducal family Degenberg the use of wheat malt for brewing beer. Wheat was reserved for the production of bread. The Purity Law allowed only the use of barley malt for brewing beer.

The family, which existed until 1602, paid considerable sums for this privilege. After the Degenbergs died out, the Bavarian dukes took over this privilege and marketed the beer very successfully.

It is the drink of choice at folk festivals and an indispensable part of local conviviality.

The malt and the brewing process differ from other types of beer. It consists of at least 50 percent wheat malt, which gives it its characteristic taste. The malt is first soaked in water to release the sugar. This sugar water is boiled. Finally, to give the brew bitterness and preservation properties, hops are added.

After boiling, the mixture is cooled, and yeast is added. The brewer's yeast used here is a special wheat beer yeast, responsible for the typical slightly banana- or clove-like spiciness. It converts sugar into alcohol and carbon dioxide. I count gingerbread and ginger as part of the flavour notes in some examples.

The brewing process itself follows traditional brewing methods, often fermenting the beverage in bottles, which is called "bottle fermentation". With wheat beer, some of the yeast often remains in the beer, contributing to its cloudy appearance.

Although the brew is drunk throughout Bavaria, there are some places that stand out. The oldest wheat beer brewery in the world still in production is the Bavarian State Brewery Weihe Stephan in Freising. Munich, with its rich beer culture and numerous breweries and beer halls, is another important place for wheat beer, especially the Schneider-Weisses-Bräuhaus.

The way it is served is different from other types of beer. It is traditionally served in tall and slender wheat beer tulips. These glasses are designed to highlight the head of foam and its bright colour. In addition, it is customary to pour slowly, swirling the rest of the bottle at the end to stir up the yeast, and then pouring it in. These enhance the flavour and cloudiness of the beer. I have to admit that I usually skip this at beer tastings.

Despite the Bavarian tradition, worldwide fans look forward to this drink. Its visual characteristics and taste make it a favourite among beer lovers. No matter how far it has travelled, wheat beer remains a piece of our culture—history, tradition, and the Bavarian way of life all in one glass.

Keller bier

The name derives from the original ageing barrels kept in the cool brewing cellars. In most cases, the beer was served directly from the barrel. Exclusively for transport, it was bottled, or stored in small barrels.

In Bavaria, it is also called Zwickelbier or Zoigl. Initially this meant the sample that the brewmaster takes from the fermentation vat before filtering. The tapping of this control with the Zwickel tap is then called "Zwickeln". Zwickel beers are more effervescent than original cellar beers. They are also more viscous because their fermentation barrels have been bunged before fermentation is complete. This allows the beer to have enough carbon dioxide and creates an elegant, frothy head. Please allow the beer to breathe sufficiently before drinking.

The name Zoigl means "sign" in the Franconian vernacular. In classic homebrewing traditions, a Zoigl was a six-pointed white star made of two triangles. Inside the structure was a beer mug or a fir branch. When such a sign hung outside a farmer's door, it was considered an invitation to all neighbours for a glass of beer (and please pay). Each triangle had its own meaning. One stood for the three elements of fire, water, and air, and the second for the ingredients malt, hops and brewing water.

It was full-bodied due to the yeast and protein presence, with an accentuated hop flavour and low carbonation. The taste of a non-plugged (capped) beer is easily recognisable in this type of beer.

This brew exhibits less beer foam. Personally, I like to let the foam sink all the way down before drinking. A serving temperature can vary depending on the manufacturer, but I usually serve at 12°C.

The colour of cellar beer ranges from deep yellow to slightly reddish. It depends on the amount of caramelised malt added. The alcohol content is about 4.5 to 5 percent. The bitter taste is around 18–25 units, and the original gravity is between 11 and 13 percent.

In my beer tastings, I like to experiment with additives such as apple juice, pear juice, or elderberry spritzers. This is a very original alternative to the Radler, which is better for quenching thirst. When choosing juices, I like to pay attention to the amount of sugar. It's better to pay a little more for good, natural juices than to risk over-sugaring.

As a drink to go with the main course, Kellerbier is great. Although I am a vegetarian, I have asked many of my non-vegetarian guests how they feel about the food pairing I recommend and can confirm that it goes very well with meat or spicy dishes. With vegetable soups and even strong goulash, I have received only positive feedback so far.

In the beer garden, I prefer this beer. However, since most beer gardens don't offer it, I go the nostalgic route and sit with my guests on the edge of the Isar River, and we have a picnic with bottled Keller bier.

Obatzda and dark bread are good accompaniments, although I prefer beers other than the dark with a cheese platter. In conclusion, keep in mind the amount of alcohol, because beers that taste just that good are very seductive.

Bock and Doppelbock

Originating in the former Hanseatic city of Einbeck in Lower Saxony, these beers are available in light or dark. They belong to the strong beers and even to the wheat beers. Top-fermented and bottom-fermented (also mixed) beers, the original wort content of which is above 16° Plato and the alcohol content from 6.5 percent.

In some references, the brewing right is associated with the granting of the city charter in 1240 by the sons of Henry the Lion for the citizens. In my research, I have not come across any children of this duke, but who knows? The first document that records Einbeck's beer trade is from 1351, when the city of Hamburg paid two pounds [avoirdupois] of money for a barrel of beer.

Bock beers had a long shelf life, which made them more desirable at the time. Linguistically, in Bavaria, one can imagine that the dialect struggled with "Eine Einbecker", which later led to "Ein Pöck" and finally simply to Bockbier. The word Starkbier is much younger, appearing only in the 20th century.

The top-fermented beer brewed in the Middle Ages was considered a luxury item and was exported over long distances, as far as Italy. To achieve the necessary shelf life, beer was brewed with a high alcohol content. For this purpose, it was mashed with an unusually high original wort content. The fermented result was a heavy, alcohol-rich beer.

The ducal court of the Wittelsbach dynasty in Munich had had beer supplied from Einbeck since 1555, until the first Bavarian Hofbräuhaus was founded in 1573, first at Trausnitz Castle in Landshut and which then moved to Munich in 1589. The aim was to brew the barley juice here. In 1614, the brewmaster Elias Pichler of Einbeck was lured away to the Hofbrau, and from then on, he brewed his Ainpöckisch beer in the capital.

Bock beers are more difficult to pair with food, as they are usually more dominant in flavour. I therefore recommend serving a smaller amount, really only as an accompaniment, because such beers are too strong. If you really want to drink it, you should not be in company, either. Therefore, for my receptions, I usually serve only 0.2 litres, usually mixed with blackberry, currant, or cherry juice in a proportion of no more than a quarter juice to three quarters beer, in appropriate wide glasses.

Bock beers are optimal at the end of an evening or with a cheese plate afterwards. Of course, the producers don't like to hear about mixing juices into their beers, but with the alcohol content, you should really moderate it.

They are also great for cooking sauces and as Christmas beer drinks. Crusted pork sauce is one of the most famous sauces in the region. Furthermore, braised bratwurst or beef goulash cooked in it are an absolute hit.

Bock beer is also a perfect ingredient for baking bread. A bread I like to bake with spelt and rye also contains Doppelbock. The dough develops much better with beer, and the flavour is also more intense.

Stark beer (Strong beer)

Beer comes in a wide variety of styles, flavours, and colours. So, it is not surprising that sometimes you hear the term "strong beer". This is not a style, but a genre of beer. Thus, all beers that have an original wort content of at least 16 percent belong to this genre. Yes, bock beers are included here, but I wanted to highlight this branch in particular.

Strong beers and bock beers were enjoyed not only at Easter, when fasting was quite strict, but also at Christmastime, when the cold weather rolled in.

This index, the original wort, is also called degree Plato. It is marked with a "P" on the beer bottle. This value not only indicates what type of beer it is, but it is also important for the beer tax. For example, the standard tax rate is 0.787 euros per hectolitre per degree Plato. In addition, a high original wort content can provide information on the alcohol content.

This type of beer has an alcohol content starting at 6.5 percent by volume, far higher than Hefeweizen beer, which only has 5.2 percent by volume, or Pilsner, which has 5.5 percent by volume.

But if most people associate beer with the German state of Bavaria, strong beer originally comes from Lower Saxony. In the Middle Ages, it was called "Bock", which was derived from the place name Einbeck (then Einböck). The "Bockbier" from this town was sold all over Germany. However, this has changed over the years, so that strong beers are now mostly drunk and brewed in Bavaria. This is how the monks brewed it here in the Middle Ages. It was mainly to satisfy hunger during the fasting period. Therefore, they used more malt and hops. Accordingly, it is called Lenten beer. It is not surprising that today, as always on 19 March, St Joseph's Day, the strong beer is tapped. Usually, this date falls in the weeks between the Shrovetide carnival and Easter, which is also Lent.

The colour of this beer is visually, with its dark brownish, or amber, to yellowish tones hardly distinguishable from other types of beer. Therefore, it is all the more important to know its own taste and to describe it in beer samples. The high original wort usually results in a sweet and malty taste. It is not uncommon to find a bitter note.

Due to the high alcohol content, it is also recommended to serve and consume small amounts of this beer. In addition, it is useful to fill the stomach at the same time. Strong beer is an outstanding companion to grilled food as well as cheese.

If the tart taste is not for you, there are options of mixing strong beer with other liquids or flavours. Since this beer already has a high alcohol content, it is recommended to use additional alcoholic beverages sparingly. For example, cola, Sprite, cherry juice, mild sparkling wine, or Fanta are best suited. For a sweeter taste experience, chocolate, caramel or even lemonade are ideal. Strong beer can be enjoyed in a punch bowl with fruit and fruit syrup.

Thus, this beer genre offers a wide range of possibilities for enjoyment.

Grutbier

Gruitbier or Grutbier is a beer that has herbs added to it. It was the most common type of beer in Europe until modern times. The grut, a mixture of herbs, was used for seasoning and fermentation. Nowadays, the term grut beer refers either to historical herbal beers or to contemporary beers that have herbs added to them. They contained and still contain hops, depending on their composition. There were several different grut blends. Typical plants for the mixture were, for example, bog myrtle, wild rosemary, bay leaf, juniper berries, elder or aniseed.

Lovers of grut beer like to use the term Urbier (original beer) in context, as it existed long before hop beer. Infusing beer with herbs, plants and spices is a technique that spans the globe. Herbal beers have been handed down in Africa and Asia as well as in Europe. In the course of modern times, hop beer prevailed over grut beer in Europe, especially in Germany.

Grutbier was the predominant beer in the Netherlands, Belgium, England, Scotland, and northern Germany in the Middle Ages. The first mentions of German Grutbier in historical sources date back to the 10th century. But the Germanic tribes also mentioned herbal beers. Historians assume that Grutbier spread from Scandinavia to Western Europe starting in the 5th century. I deepened my knowledge of this environment when I wrote my novel, *Markgraf Iron*. Around the Grut developed craft and the Grutrecht. The collection, preparation and drying of herbs were separate crafts in the production of grut beer.

Brewers were obliged to buy and use only the specified grut. The Grutherr (grut master) was responsible for the supervision of the Grut and assigned the rights as well as the Grut. With the allocation of grut rights and the control of grut houses, the business surrounding grut beer developed into an important regional economic factor.

Grut beers taste different depending on the composition of the grut. Depending on the herbs chosen, they have a bitter, spicy, or floral taste. Fermentation results in a slightly sour aroma. Besides the grut, the production influences the taste. The grut came, depending on the method, during the wort's boiling, fermentation, or maturation.

The composition of the herbs varied from region to region. Therefore, in addition to Grutbier, the terms Gagel (bog myrtle) and Porst (wild rosemary) are also common for this beer variant. They then refer specifically to the herbal ingredients. Compared to grut beer, hop-based beer is more durable and less expensive. From the 14th century, hop beers began to spread in Germany.

The two beer varieties co-existed until modern times, when the Purity Law led to the decline of herbal beer in Germany. In that sense, gruit beer was the Neanderthal. In Bavaria, for example, gruit beers were known until then as Greuzenich or Gräussing.

With the German Purity Law of 1516, issued by the Bavarian dukes Wilhelm IV and Ludwig X, the decline of herbal beers began. Initially, the restriction of beers to the brewing ingredients barley, hops and water applied only to the Duchy of Bavaria.

In other regions, herb beers lasted longer until the Purity Law became law throughout Germany in 1906. From then on, beer spiked with herbs was banned because of the ingredients that were not allowed.

In countries such as Belgium or the Netherlands, gruit beer remained, but lost importance during the modern era due to the triumph of hops.

In the present day, there are various breweries in Germany, such as the Lahnsteiner Brewery, that are once again dedicated to herbal beer. The Lahnsteiner Brewery in Rhineland-Palatinate produces a wide variety of beers, among which Grutbier is just one.

A well-known Gruthaus brewery is run by Philipp Overberg in Münster. He is trying to revive traditions and develop new grut beers. For example, the Grutbier called Dubbel Porse is based on reconstructed historical Münster recipes.

One of the ingredients for grut is bog myrtle. The plant was one of the most common ingredients for grut beers in the Middle Ages. Today it is protected in Germany because of its rarity, so it is imported from Scotland.

Another well-known representative of German grut beers is Pia Morgenroth with the G. broi brand, whose beers are produced in Berlin and Saxony. With these, the designation herbal beer is appropriate, as they contain nettle or yarrow and dispense with hops.

In contrast to Germany, Grutbier as an herbal beer has never ceased to exist in other countries. Especially in the Netherlands, Belgium and the USA, there are still breweries that produce grut beer.

Among beer lovers, a return to and recognition of old beer varieties is beginning. Interested parties and hobby brewers initiated the International Gruit Day, which takes place annually on 1 February. Initially, it was mainly an occasion to discuss gruit beer at meetings or via social media. Now, breweries participate in events to mark Gruit Day.

Some variants of gruit beer are fruitier or very mild in alcohol, which is perfectly in line with the trend in the market.

Since gruit beer does not comply with the beer laws in force in Germany, it is considered a craft beer. Special permits are required to brew beers that do not comply with German beer laws. These are bureaucratic and financially costly, so some German grut beers are produced abroad and then imported back into Germany.

The only German state that does not allow exceptions is Bavaria. No grut beer brewery will be setting up here anytime soon, but that doesn't mean it's impossible. In the time I've been involved with beer as a sommelier, I've seen a trend toward more variety and independence on the market, which is also a reason for the younger generation to try new ways.

The wisdom of women

... we have no more time for further searching and thinking - our food is running out, especially our beer supplies - from the logbook of the Mayflower 1620.

For me, a special concern on the subject of beer is to document, or even highlight, the mistakes in the development of society in connection with women. Brewing beer was a woman's business. Several sources prove that especially the Catholic Church, with its greed for money, unjustly accused many women of witchcraft in order to eliminate the competition. It should be mentioned that even Hildegard of Bingen was a victim of this.

Beer has been under the protection of goddesses since the beginning of mankind. The oldest goddess who protected brewing is considered to be the Sumerian deity Ninkasi. Among the Romans, it was Ceres, the goddess of agriculture and fertility, who also protected brewers. Among the Egyptians, Tjenemit was the goddess of creation and responsible for brewing beer. The Hathor Festival should also not be forgotten. This was where in Egypt two weeks of boozing and rowdiness took place.

Who could think that this country was once so lascivious?

Beer has played an important role in human history in connection with religious rituals. In some religions, providing only the best for the gods during ceremonies meant using an alcoholic beverage.

Excavations in Egypt or Europe showed that beer was used in rituals as an offering or as a burial gift, and the priests in the church also enjoyed wine.

In Finnish myths, it is a woman who invents beer: According to the national epic Kalevala, which translated the oral sagas into writing, Osmotar invented beer by mixing barley, hops and water with honey.

Literary and archaeological traditions suggest that in many cultures, women were responsible for brewing beer. The best example is the Vikings, where brewing beer was the responsibility of women. Possibly because of this, the figure of Heidrun was made female.

It is known that the witch's hut had nothing to do with witchcraft but acted as an advertising board for the brewers. With it, blithe ladies lured the market visitors to their freshly brewed beer. They had to have the kettles bubbling in their sheds outside the town. Many such women were single and defenceless against the church and its agents. The broom with the head down indicated that the hut was swept, and guests could be received (witches' broom). In Europe, brewing beer was the responsibility of women until modern times. Brewing was part of the household chores, with which additional money could be earned. One of the oldest breweries in the country run by women was located in Erfurt, for example, in an Ursuline convent. Evidence shows that nuns there produced beer on a large scale in the 16th century, and not just for their own consumption. The most famous German nuns who brewed beer were Hildegard von Bingen in the 12th century and

Katharina von Bora in the 16th century. Women mixed additives into the beers to enhance the flavour, as I recommend in my blends. They used fancy marketing strategies to try to advertise special qualities in their products.

Hair growth on the chest, fertility and virility were some of the promises that drew customers to their houses. Heavy marketing by brewers drowned out this past, calling on consumers to consume absurd amounts of the beverage. This is despite the fact that doctors, nutritionists, and the human mind all unanimously say that drinking a litre of beer is beyond what is humanly possible and extremely harmful. It may be funny for young people, but when we all choke on the cost of health insurance in old age, we will have no support from brewers and even less from the Catholic Church.

Cats as companions of these poor people were also persecuted by the Catholic Church. The decree Summis desiderantes affectibus by Pope Innocent VIII in 1484 shows that our society has been misguided, and we should really thoroughly reconsider customs like Halloween. Women are not witches, and cats, snakes and dogs are not ambassadors of hell. Hildegard von Bingen viewed beer primarily from a health perspective and recommended its consumption for various ailments. She championed hop beer, which had not been widely consumed until then, and she preferred it. Without her, we would have only bland and short-lived beer. When I search the old recipes and find misjudgements several times in the history of beer, it reinforces my views. We need a new, independent perspective on enjoyment based less on quantity and more on quality.

Katharina von Bora learned to brew during her time as a nun, and she also cultivated it as the wife of Martin Luther. She did it not just for fun but to supplement the household budget. In Luther's letters, it can be read that she brewed far more than the usual household consumption. Money, however, was the bone of contention between women and the church. As brewing became more professional, men and organised companies prevailed over women brewers. A professional beer trade and guilds for brewers and maltsters emerged. Thus, especially in Europe, women lost their importance (and their lives) in the brewing trade. At the time of the witch hunts, the phenomenon of beer witches was added: they were witches who allegedly poisoned beer or made it spoil. Women who brewed liquids in cauldrons were now suspected of making witches' potions. As with many witchcraft accusations, the so-called beer witches were often the victims of resourceful competitors. As the Reformation progressed, an image of women as limited to the home and family became entrenched. Women who produced beer for sale or served it at a market did not fit into this patriarchal role model. The centres of beer brewing became monasteries and professional breweries. Some women successfully ran breweries, but mostly as widows who took over their husbands' inheritance. These included Therese Wagner in Bavaria, for example, or Fanny Leicht in Baden-Württemberg. Susanna Waitzinger also led a brewery to success. She managed the Waitzinger Brewery in Miesbach in the 19th century. She took over this task during the lifetime of her husband, who, according to rumours and lore, was not very enterprising. When he died, she expanded the brewery and the inn to include a hotel. In this way, she achieved making her brewery at that time one of the largest private breweries in Upper Bavaria.

I thank these women, who have left something in our history, and I regret that an apology for the numerous crimes is still pending. I am sure that now is also a good time for new visions in the beer world. And also, Heidrun is a woman, albeit on four legs; without her, I could not have written this book.

Possibilities of brewing

Who does not know the saying "good beer is not mixed", although we occupy bread with all kinds? Both foods are made of the same ingredients, except for hops. Berliner Weisse is extremely sour, like the neighbouring Belgian brew. There, it is after all out of the question to mix these beers with woodruff, raspberry juice, cherry liqueur, or other juices. St. Hildegard von Bingen already wrote in her medical notes that beer (especially spelt beer) is an excellent carrier medium for medicinal herbs.

Those who drink alcohol should always drink water to compensate. With this premise in mind, years ago, I started looking for methods to mix the beer to reduce alcohol. In Bavaria, we have our Radler, and many breweries are constantly looking for non-alcoholic variants that provide refreshment and enjoyment.

Hemp as a complementary plant to hops is understood as an aphrodisiac. In fact, hops have a rather restraining effect. Given the celibacy and other absurd restrictions of Catholicism, it would be unthinkable for hemp to be widely accepted. Since other herbs have better medicinal properties that are also beneficial to health, they should not be dispensed with. A well-hopped pilsner before sleep works wonders, as the saying goes.

Our stomach has an average volume of 1.5 litres. No one is fit to drive after a measure of beer. The decomposition of alcohol depends on the constitution and gender of the drinker, body size, but should not more than 200 ml per hour.

This means that you need to be sober for at least two hours to be able to drive a vehicle again.

The portion offered would even be incitement to a crime, but since big corporations and a lot of money are behind it, the courts put the responsibility on the consumers.

Nettle, another variety of gruit beer, is harvested only once a year. That is why it is particularly appreciated for brewing or preparing elixirs. The natural taste offers a spring-like note to complement it. As an accompanying effect, the various healing properties of the herb can be added to the moment of enjoyment.

The production of nettle beer follows a recipe that requires only a few ingredients: fresh nettle leaves, lemon juice, water, honey or sugar and brewer's yeast. After boiling the leaves and adding the rest of the ingredients, the whole thing must ferment for three to six days.

The young beer is bottled in sterilised swing-top bottles and kept at rest for seven days. After a maturation period of one to two weeks, the result is ready to be enjoyed.

The elixir follows the same recipe, but without brewer's yeast and water; a fermentation period is then unnecessary. Nettle beer lacks a head.

It has a subtle sweetness accompanied by a refreshing herbal note. Overall, the result is a delicately spicy flavour with notes of iron and citrus.

For several years now, small breweries have been reviving the old recipes and flair of the past, seeking innovative and delicious products.

Beer tasting at home.

1) So far, we have described some types of beer. You should do the same for your own beer tasting. Drinking without conversation is really bland.

2) I recited the history of Bavaria, but you can describe your country, neighbourhood, or family. This is an excellent introduction to the evening, and then prepare the table.

3) The glasses should be wide, conducive to breathing, and have a long stem.

4) Water should be served between beers.

5) Bread is usually included in my beer samples, but you can do without it.

6) Bring the beer to the appropriate serving temperature.

7) Never serve more than 125 ml.

8) Possibly supplement the beer with juices or elixirs.

9) Distribute rating sheets.

10) Change glasses if possible.

My recommendation for a balanced beer drink mix is to add one-third of the elixir or herbal beer to one beer. It is, in short, a glass of magic.

Heidrun has accomplished many things here and has clearly earned a beer.

The facts described here are historically proven. Where, in my opinion, it allows an interpretation, I have formulated it accordingly, so that there are no misunderstandings. Have fun with my recommendations and send me your opinion and experiences. You can always learn, and if not, then there was too much beer.